LEARN ABOUT
CLOUDS

by Golriz Golkar

Published by The Child's World®
1980 Lookout Drive • Mankato, MN 56003-1705
800-599-READ • www.childsworld.com

Design Elements: Shutterstock Images
Photographs ©: KC Lens and Footage/Shutterstock Images,
cover (clouds), 1 (clouds); Shutterstock Images, cover
(jar), 1 (jar), 4 (hair spray), 4 (ice cubes), 10, 13, 17, 21, 23;
Elizabeth A. Cummings/Shutterstock Images, 4 (food coloring);
Rick Orndorf, 5; DGL Images/iStockphoto, 6; Detchana
Wangkheeree/Shutterstock Images, 9; iStockphoto, 14; Jan
Cieslicki/Shutterstock Images, 18

ISBN 9781503832138
LCCN 2018962815

Printed in the United States of America
PA02420

About the Author

Golriz Golkar is a teacher and
children's author who lives
in Nice, France. She enjoys
cooking, traveling, and looking
for ladybugs on nature walks.

TABLE OF CONTENTS

CHAPTER 1

Let's Make a Cloud!

MATERIALS
- ☐ One cup of boiling water
- ☐ Blue food coloring
- ☐ Glass jar with lid
- ☐ Ice cubes
- ☐ Hair spray

It is a good idea to gather your materials before you begin.

After you spray the hair spray, a cloud forms!

STEPS

1. With an adult's help, heat the water until it boils. Let it cool for one minute. Add a few drops of blue food coloring.

2. Pour the water into the jar. Swirl it around to warm up the glass.

5

Be careful with the hot water.
Ask an adult if you need help.

3. Turn the jar lid upside down. Place the ice cubes on it.

4. Keep the lid upside down. Place it on top of the jar. Wait about ten seconds.

5. Lift the lid. Spray the hair spray very quickly into the jar.

6. Put the lid back immediately.

7. Watch a cloud form! Wait two minutes. Remove the lid. Watch the cloud escape.

CHAPTER 2

How Do Clouds Form?

Air contains an invisible gas called **water vapor**. It forms when water on Earth is heated. The water becomes too hot to stay a liquid. It turns into water vapor. It releases into the sky. This process is called **evaporation**.

Clouds are formed from water vapor in the air.

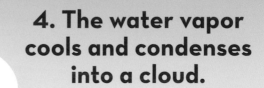

4. The water vapor cools and condenses into a cloud.

3. Water vapor rises into cooler air.

1. Sunlight warms Earth's surface.

2. Water begins to evaporate.

Cloud Formation

Clouds are constantly forming as water heats up and cools.

Water vapor moves up in the **atmosphere**. The vapor cools the air. Water vapor changes form when air is cool enough. This happens through **condensation**. Water vapor attaches to tiny particles. They include dust, ice, sea salt, or similar particles. Either tiny water droplets or ice crystals are formed. This depends on the temperature and **altitude** in the atmosphere.

Water droplets form in warm temperatures. Colder temperatures mean the water freezes into ice. Higher altitudes are colder than lower altitudes. Many water droplets or ice crystals combine to form clouds.

Clouds can be formed from tiny ice crystals sticking together.

Condensation can also be seen on cold drinks.
The cold surface causes the water vapor
in the air to cool and turn into drops.

The hair spray was the condensation particle in the glass jar experiment. The ice cooled the air inside the jar. The hot water inside released water vapor. The vapor condensed when it touched the hair spray particles. A cloud formed.

DID YOU KNOW?

There are clouds in outer space. Mars has clouds like those found above Earth. On Jupiter and Venus, the clouds are made of dangerous gases.

CHAPTER 3

Why Are Clouds Important?

Clouds play an important role in weather. Water droplets and ice particles combine to form larger drops. They fall from clouds as **precipitation.** Precipitation includes rain, snow, hail, and sleet. It is part of the planet's water cycle. The planet would not have water without it. Life on Earth would be impossible.

Precipitation, such as rain, is an important part of Earth's water cycle.

Clouds can help cool temperatures ⋰
down by blocking the sun.

Clouds also help control Earth's
temperatures. They hold in heat to keep
the planet warm at night. They provide
shade and cooler temperatures during
the day.

Air pollution from cars and factories can change weather patterns. Dust particles condense water vapor. Heavy rainfall can occur in cities with warm temperatures. Too much rain can cause damage and interrupt life cycles on Earth.

CHAPTER 4

What Kinds of Clouds Are There?

Stratus clouds are low-level clouds. They look like flat sheets.

Altostratus clouds are also flat. Cumulus (KYOO-myuh-luss) clouds look like fluffy cotton balls. Both kinds are midlevel clouds. They mean possible rain.

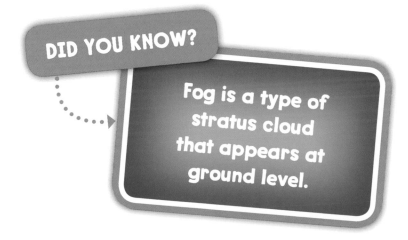

DID YOU KNOW?

Fog is a type of stratus cloud that appears at ground level.

The direction of cirrus clouds shows which way the wind is blowing.

Cumulus clouds become thunderclouds when they rise higher and grow bigger.

Cirrus (SEER-us) clouds are thin, wispy clouds made of ice. They are high in the sky. Cirrus clouds do not produce rain.

Glossary

altitude (AL-ti-tood) Altitude is the height of anything above earth or sea level. Airplanes fly at a very high altitude.

atmosphere (AT-mos-feer) The atmosphere is the gases surrounding the earth; the air. Air pollution releases harmful chemicals into the atmosphere.

condensation (con-den-SAY-shun) Condensation is the process of turning from gas to liquid. Water vapor turns into liquid water through condensation.

evaporation (ee-vap-o-RAY-shun) Evaporation is the process of turning from liquid into gas. Liquid water turns into water vapor through evaporation.

precipitation (pre-sip-i-TAY-shun) Precipitation is water falling in the form of rain, snow, hail, or sleet. The weather forecast often predicts precipitation.

water vapor (WAH-ter VAY-pur) Water vapor is water in the form of gas. When water is boiled, water vapor forms.

To Learn More

In the Library

Jensen, Belinda. *Weather Clues in the Sky: Clouds.*
Minneapolis, MN: Millbrook Press, 2016.

Morgan, Emily. *Next Time You See a Cloud.*
Arlington, VA: NSTA Kids, 2016.

Pope, Kristen. *What Is the Difference Between Clouds and Fog?* Mankato, MN: The Child's World, 2017.

On the Web

Visit our website for links about clouds:
childsworld.com/links

Note to Parents, Teachers, and Librarians: We routinely verify our Web links to make sure they are safe and active sites. So encourage your readers to check them out!

Index